Contents

POLITICAL FUNDING IN INDIA: A CRITICAL ANALYSIS IF REPRESENTATION OF PEOPLE'S ACT, 1951

VOLUME 1, ISSUE 4 OF BRILLOPEDIA

AISHWARYA VATSA

ISBN 979-888530913-4

Preface

"Start writing, no matter what. The water does not flow until the faucet is turned on".

-Louis L'Amour

Hundreds of students and professors are contributing their work to Brillopedia, we are here to provide ample information about Law and Contemporary issues. Our aim is to provide a platform for today's generation to express their views and ideas on law and contemporary law.

Publication

This research paper is published in volume 1, issue 4 of Brillopedia

CHAPTER ONE

Abstract

Political funds are imperative to run the party democracy. All the political parties generate funds for various purposes. A political party runs like an organisation, which has both fixed and variable costs of management.There are some essential and unavoidable costs that a party has to bear for itsday-to-day functioning, related to offices, staff expenses, vehicles used, meetings and others too. But, there are added intricacies for the obvious reasons. The matter which involves money is never generally a cakewalk. The trust built on public institutions is most necessary and must be maintained. Such belief in system and democracy has kept us binding together and inefficiency of such institution makes the society unstable. The paper attempts to look into the Representation of Peoples Act, 1951, Constitution of India, The Vohra (Committee) Report, 1993, and other related laws and aims to identify the legal lacuna and subsequent solutions for the same.

Keywords: Election, Representation of Peoples'Act, Political Funding, Democracy

If we attempt to look into the background of political funding there are some interesting facts to be presented. There were efficient policies in context to political funding during the Nehru reign. But the corruption issue was rampant back then too. The roots of corruption in Congress existed in pre-independence era. Mahatma Gandhi himself had passed a remark in 1939 that "I would go to the length of giving the whole Congress a decent burial, rather than put up with the corruption that is rampant"[1]. During Nehru's governance in India, corporates were allowed to make donations which was called premium for "Political Insurance". The author does not presume the thought of the then Prime Minister, but he openly defended his ministers tainted with corruption charges. In a report submitted over public administration in 1951 by A.D.Gorwala made a snarky remark that-

"the government went out of its way to shield its (corrupt) ministers".[2] There was infamous Jeep scandal where wide corruption allegations were levied against V K Krishna Menon in the purchase of Jeeps for the Indian Army. The government not just only defended Menon, but also denied judicial enquiry into it. Menon was shortly appointed as Minister without portfolio.[3] The Congress party enjoyed a sort of monopoly as political giant hence was flooded with funds.

Tables started to turn with the arrival of Swatantra Party in 1959 which had something better to offer. It furnished priority to freedom over equality which shook the foundation of Nehru's socialism. It talked about free enterprise concept and less taxes for corporates. These widened its popularity as it started to get a lot corporate funding as support. This went well till late 60s which made Indira Gandhi concerned about the situation. She in order to confront this problem blocked the way of corporate funding in politics and banned it. Followed by the period of emergency, which is another story to tell. Power makes one corrupt and Congress could not be aloof from it. The license and permit Raj began and hard cash used to play the significant part in congress coffers. The corporates who did not agree were forced to agree to the laid terms by the government. In the year 1985, the then PM Rajeev Gandhi lifted the ban over political funding but the damage was done in the context of development of black economy[4]. Mr Gandhi regime too was filled with corruption and scams followed by MR P V Narshimarao tenure. Post such unfortunate incidents the legislature woke up and realised that there is urgent need for Party funding regulation. The Election Commission had requested some reforms through a proposal in the year 1982 and again in 1986.Before they could implement such reformative measures the V P Singh government had fallen. Butt over the coming years few of the reforms got included in the regulation. The plea of the election commission to include contributions of friends or parties in calculating the ceiling of election expenditure by a candidate was never considered. In 1997, I.K Gujral's cabinet raised the ceiling from Rs 6 lakhs to Rs. 15 lakhs.[5] The candidate had to furnish Expenditure details and these were supposed to be matched with the returns of the parties. This was one of the most significant changes brought during that time. In 1996 there was a Supreme Court judgment under Common Cause v. Union of India[6] that mandated corporates to furnish full details of funding in public domain.

This was the historical background on the matter of political funding. It's not that the governments did not take steps at all. There have been reports furnished by several committees established to look into the domain of electoral reformation. Further, we will discuss the key points of all such committees and their recommendations. That will help us to track down the seriousness of the government to bring about substantial change. Elections are backbone of any healthy democracy because it is the only way we can voluntarily choose our representatives. These chosen people have the most important job in hand, that is, legislation. If this sectionis compromised,the electoral structure might get highly damaged. The Election Commission and Law commission both have expressed their concerns over the irregularities found on the ground as well as legislation put forth.

Various politicians and candidates openly criticise the low threshold of expenditure enforced by law and also demand its revision. These candidates blame Election Commission of India for such legislation in place. But the reality remains different. Election Commission is merely a recommendatory body as far as legislation is concerned. The concerns about such limits are purely dealt by the legislature and government. The fact however is that these limits are fixed by the Ministry of Law and Justice, Legislative Department under the Conduction of Election Rules.[7] It suggests that government is the only entity that can amend such rules and regulations. The political leaders and candidates openly say that due to these limits there is always a sense of intricacy. They claim that the laid limit on expenditure is generally crossed by those contesting the election. Some may argue that these limits are useless in nature but excessive flow of money if not checked would the democratic structure of this country.

Such influence of money was publicly known but it came officially into light after publication of Vohra Committee[8] findings. Mr N.N. Vohra, the then Union Home Secretary, quoted reports from the Central Bureau of Investigation, "An organized crime Syndicate/Mafia generally commences its activities by indulging in petty crime at the local level, mostly relating to illicit distillation/gambling/organized satta and prostitution in the larger towns. In port towns, their activities involve smuggling and sale of imported goods and progressively graduate to narcotics and drug trafficking. In the bigger cities, the main source of income relates to real estate – forcibly occupying lands/buildings, procuring such properties at cheap rates by forcing out the existing occupants/tenants etc. Overtime, the money power thus acquired is used for building up contacts with bureaucrats, politicians, and expansion of activities with impunity. The money power is used to develop a network of muscle-power, which is also used by the politicians during elections.... The nexus between the criminal gangs, police, bureaucracy and politicians has come out clearly in various parts of the country"[9].

This kind of reports slams the system to the very end. The machineries of state which are supposed to helping in conducting free and fair elections were always in nexus of such illicit people for the reasons best known to them. These kinds of situation make the public helpless and they are forced to vote such candidates who are really not fit for the job. The executive of this country is enveloped by corruption and legislative pressure as there is no strict separation of power structure in this country. There is also a need to curb the high cost of campaigning to provide a level playing field for anyone who wants to contest elections.[10]

Let us look into the perspective of funding by taking into account the related legislation in place. Section 77(1) and 78 of RPA[11] read with rule 86 mandates to maintain the true account of their electoral expenses and also file the same with the district officer in place. The Supreme Court in a landmark judgment of Dalchand Jain v Narayan Shankar Trivedi[12], held that incorrect maintenance would not attract the provisions of corrupt practices unless the expenditures are within the laid limits. Further in the leading case of PUCL v. Union of India, the court recommended a measure laid down in NCRWC[13] report and stated that, "The Commission recommends that the political parties as well as individual candidates be made subject to a proper statutory audit of the amounts they spend.... At the end of the election each candidate should submit an audited statement of expenses under specific heads. EC should devise specific formats for filing such statements so that fudging of accounts becomes difficult. Also, the audit should not only be mandatory but it should be enforced by the Election Commission."

As we know that there is absence of limit over expense by political parties for running their desired program, parties must follow the limit laid in section 77(3)[14] and Rule 90, of Election Rules, 1961 while furnishing financial assistance to contesting candidates for the purpose of election campaigns. These amounts shall only be paid by a crossed account payee cheque or draft or bank transfer, and never by liquid money. As far as auditing is concerned all political parties must maintain appropriate books of accounts[15] which shall be based on the guidelines issued by the Institute of Chartered Accountants of India (ICAI) in order to calculate the party income. These books of accounts must be audited and reviewed by the registered chartered Accountant and must be submitted annually before the stipulated time period. These rules and regulations are put in there for a purpose and these timely audits are compulsory in nature with attached sanctions.

[1]HT Correspondent, *Congress culture is 'anti-thesis of Gandhian thought': PM Modi*, HINDUSTAN TIMES (July 12, 2019 12:28 IST), https://www.hindustantimes.com/india-news/congress-culture-is-anti-thesis-of-gandhian-thought-pm-modi/story-XWrIDHJf0PhpxGfRNOacEI.html

[2]Kiran J Prakash, *Political Party funding and Corruption*, LOKSATTA, (December 16, 2005),

https://www.fdrindia.org/old/publications/PoliticalPartyFunding.pdf

[3]*ibid*

[4]*ibid*

[5]*ibid*

[6]Common Cause v. Union of India, JT 1996 (3) 706

[7]Rule 90, Conduction of Election Rules 1961

[8]The Vohra (Committee) Report, 1993, Ministry of Home Affairs, Government of India

[9]*ibid*

[10]NileshEkka, Electoral Reforms in India - Issues and Reforms, Association for Democratic Reform.(ADR)

[11]Representations of People Act, 1951, No. 43, Act of Parliament, 1951 (India)

[12]Dalchand Jain v Narayan Shankar Trivedi (1969) 3 SCC 685

[13]National Commission to Review Working Constitution (NCRWC) , 2002

[14]Supra note 11, S.77(3)

[15]Section 13 A, Income Tax Act, 1961, No. 43, Acts of Parliament, 1961 (India)

CHAPTER TWO

Laws regulating disclosure of political contribution by parties and companies

Section 29C[1] takes into account the disclosure of funding accumulated by political parties and also mandates every party to furnish an annual report against of all contributions exceeding Rs. 2000, received on behalf a person or company, and submits such report to the Election Commission. If this particular law remain not complied with, the party fail to get entitlement to any such tax benefit against Section 29C (4)[2] read with Section 13A of the IT Act[3]. The Supreme Court has observed in the case of Gajanan Krishnaji Bapat v Dattaji Raghobaji Meghe[4] that, "We wish, however, to point out that though the practice followed by political parties in not maintaining accounts of receipts of the sale of coupons and donations as well as the expenditure incurred in connection with the election of its candidate appears to be a reality but it certainly is not a good practice. It leaves a lot of scope for soiling the purity of election by money influence."[5]

Section 182(3) of The Companies Act, 2013[6] has the responsibility to regulate the disclosure of political contribution on behalf of companies, mandating each company to furnish the total sum of its donation, and the also name of the party for which the said contribution is being done, in every financial year in its profit and loss account. Section 75A[7] of the RPA mandates each and every elected candidate in a parliamentary constituency to furnish relevant details against their assets and liabilities to the Lower House Speaker or the Rajya Sabha Chairperson within ninety days of taking the oath for their seat in Parliament.

These are some of the most significant legislation controlling and putting check on the gross abuse of money power. Although there are legislative limitation capping election expense for a candidates and regulating the furnished detail of donations by companies to political parties, the same is not efficiently governed, either due legislative incompetence, or failure of law enforcement. NCRWC electoral recommendations made a shocking revelation that general expenditure actually incurred by the candidates exceeds twenty to thirty times.[8] In fact, one of the major concerns regarding expenditure and contribution regulation is that the apparently low ceiling of candidate expenditure increases the demand for black money cash contributions and drives campaign expenditure underground, causing parties to conceal their actual source of funds and expenditure.[9]

[1] Supra note 11, S.29 C

[2] Supra note 11, S. 29 C(4)

[3]The Information Technology Act, 2000, No. 21, Act of Parliament, 2000 (India)

[4]Gajanan Krishnaji Bapat v Dattaji Raghobaji Meghe (1995) 5 SCC 347

[5] *ibid*

[6]The Companies Act, 2013, No. 18, Act of Parliament, 2013(India)

[7]Supra note 11, S. 75A

[8]A Consultation Paper on Review of Election Law, Processes, and Reform Options, NCRWC(January 2001)

[9]M.V. Rajeev Gowda & E. Sridharan, *Reforming India's Party Financing and Election Expenditure Laws*, 11(2) ELECTION L.J. 226,p. 232-35 (2012)

[10]Supra note 11, S. 77

CHAPTER THREE

Legislative Irregularities

There are series of legal loopholes related to election expenditure, which opens the window for corruption. First, and the most significantly, despite the Election and Other Related Laws (Amendment) Act 2003, section 77[1] of the Act does only cover candidates' not political parties. It is like keeping the monster free and chasing insignificant rat. The political parties are the entities which are making and spending large chunk of money eventually making election hell lot expensive. The provision calls for maintenance of separate account for all the election related expenditure from the date of nomination till the end of declaration. Due to this reason the political parties and its supporters are given free hand to spend on promotion of the party until and unless it is not used to support a particular candidate.

The impact of section 77(1) is clearly visible in the election commission handbook. The Election Commission categorises the election advertisement under three heads.

i. "Expenditure on general party propaganda seeking support for the party and its candidates in general, but, without any reference to any particular candidate or any particular class/group of candidates.
ii. Expenditure incurred by the party, in advertisements etc., directly seeking support and / or vote for any particular candidate or group of candidates.
iii. Expenditure incurred by the party, which can be related to the expenditure for promoting the prospects of any particular candidate or group of candidates."

According to the rules of Election Commission the first abovementioned instance is does not get included under section 77 but later two points are well covered under it.[2] Secondly the clever party candidates can manage the accounting in such way to adjust candidate's expense as the expense on party leaders in order to avail the exception to section 77[3]. The law states that if leader of the party is travelling through as star campaigner to other parts of territory for the promotion of the party, then all such expense of travel would not be included under the purview of law. The legislature has kept these kinds of loopholes around the law to facilitate itself. If a person is authorised to make law for himself he would definitely unreasonably mess with it in bad way. So did the political parties in power and no one is there to put an objection to it.

The scope of Section 77(1) is not very wide as it extends only from the date of filing of nomination till the end day declaration and thus any expenses made in the left out period do enjoy exemption from any kind of cap or law. Another significant lacuna can be obtained out in section 182(1) of companies Act.[4]For authorisation for donation of political parties there is need of a resolution passed by the board of directors. The decision to donate such huge amounts of funds to the political parties being decided by a bunch of people and not the shareholders is a point of concern.[5] The shareholders are the real owners of the company and there shall be there inclusion in such huge decision making process.

The disclosure laws need further strengthening. Election Commission of India transparency guidelines is a form of toothless tiger with no attached sanction over its defiance. Unlike other countries the political candidates files their return with the Election Commission not online on any website. There is utmost need for people to know about the candidates so that they can make an informed decision. This is of utmost importance to bring about transparency in the public domain and inform the voters with the relevant information regarding candidate, donors, and expenditures of a political party.

We must keep in mind that voting is a form of expression that a citizen has a fundamental right to do. A voter has right to elect his or her desired candidate on the basis of his preferred choices. Right to freedom of expression is under Article 19(1) (a)[6] of Indian constitution. It only extends to citizens and natural persons, and corporations have not been considered citizens with free speech rights[7] but shareholders may exercise such right.[8] Hence one can argue that a company does not enjoy free expression to donate politically without the involvement of shareholders. There are other major lacunas in context of recent amendments made in series of laws to facilitate anonymous funding to the political parties. A public Interest Litigation has been filed in the Supreme Court on the matter and verdict is still awaited.

[1]Supra note 11, S. 77

[2] ECI, Instructions on Expenditure Monitoring in Elections

[3]Supra note 11, S. 77(1)

[4]Supra note 21, S. 182(1)

[5]SamyaChatterjee, *Campaign Finance Reforms in India: Issues and Challenges*, ORF ISSUE BRIEF #47, (December 2012)

[6]The Constitution of India, 1950, A. 19(1)(a)

[7]State Trading Corporation v. CTO AIR 1963 SC 1811

[8]Divisional Forest Officer v Bishwanath Tea Company AIR 1981 SC 1368

CHAPTER FOUR

Conclusion

By looking at the laws of different countries there comes a general feeling that why do not we adopt such methods which seriously works on the way to fair election? This is serious question to answer. We must not presume that others nations are managing elections better than us. A law in place does not indicate its being practiced seriously. In the recent United States election there were made credible allegation with big interference made at the end of Russia.[1] This made headlines and lot of debates were done. Despite the laws things do not get in place correctly. The people in power are always mightier and they love to twist and turn legal hemisphere. When we compare different jurisdictions with India, we can very well deduce the positive highlights. Some of the steps could be integrated in our system which could include short period of campaign, complete ban on foreign funding, controlled usage of social media, reasonable limit on corporate donations, limit on political party expenditure etc. All these novel steps will equalise the playing field for every candidate. It is our constitutional right to contest election but absence of equal treatment discourages a normal citizen for such participation. If we intend to make a robust democratic system, involvement of people is mandatory in a positive way. In another spat, from time to the subject of Electronic Voting Machine credibility has been in continuously in question by the political parties and civil liberty organisations.[2]These matters should be looked into because this is the backbone of democracy. People make their choice and they must not an ounce of doubt in their mind about their contribution.

Various political parties and democratic organisations have objected to the attitude of Election Commission which seems quite premeditated. The commission has denied all such claims relating to EVMs from time to time and ignored the matter taking it just as political nuance.[3] There has been credible allegation over the commission for its selective actions and punishment for the violators. In the 2019 general election, there were communal speeches given by prominent leaders but actions were taken on selective leaders. The Election Commission is an independent body and must act like one. It is a concrete fact that the commission has been levied with insufficient power which makes it nearly impossible to conduct free and fair election. Lately, Delhi Election 2020 saw a lot of turmoil as various communal and derogatory statements were passed and the commission's role was next to negligible.[4]The election related laws are never enforced the way they are expected to rather administration turns a blind eye towards such incidents. Inflow of large amount of unaccounted money and their foul use has led to destruction of our social and legal fabric. The Commission must show it's the highest integral standard and must overview the whole procedure efficiently. The trust built on public institutions is most necessary and must be maintained. Hence the commission must restore the lost faith of people and continuously strife towards balanced democratic system.

[1]Jonathan Masters, *Russia, Trump, and the 2016 U.S. Election*, Council on Foreign Relation, February 26, 2018https://www.cfr.org/backgrounder/russia-trump-and-2016-us-election

[2] Press Trust of India, *Oppn parties raise concerns over reports of alleged EVM tampering; Pranab also steps in,*(May 21, 2019 20:21 IST)

https://www.business-standard.com/article/pti-stories/oppn-parties-raise-concerns-over-reports-of-alleged-evm-tampering-pranab-also-steps-in-119052101461_1.html

[3]Pallavi, *The many claims of EVM tampering in India,* India Today, (January 21, 2019 19:48 IST)

https://www.indiatoday.in/elections/story/the-many-claims-of-evm-tampering-in-india-1435638-2019-01-21

[4]TanvirAeijaz, *Making sense of the 2020 Delhi elections*, East Asia Forum,(20 March 2020)

https://www.eastasiaforum.org/2020/03/20/making-sense-of-the-2020-delhi-elections/

www.ingramcontent.com/pod-product-compliance
Ingram Content Group UK Ltd.
Pitfield, Milton Keynes, MK11 3LW, UK
UKHW021926190726
13853UKWH00002B/870

9 798885 309134